"I don't know anyone who is as knowledgeable about tea and all the benefits as Jenny Tse. Jenny inspires us all to live a life to strive for strong health through the ancient ways of natural healing. If you have something missing in your life, you are going to want to read Jenny's book. It's a must read in today's 'clean' times."

~ Lori Packee,
Sipping Streams Customer

"Remarkable life journey from athletics to tea education, entrepreneur, winner of international tea awards and much more. 'I can't, but you can do everything, Jenny!' Inspiring personal story interwoven with fascinating tea information."

~ Shalini Agarwal
Glenburn Tea Estate

"The energy Jenny Tse has for her brainchild, Sipping Streams Tea Company is unparalleled! And now, this amazing book sharing with us her journey to reach this point. The tea she created for us, 1,000 Mile Tea, has become a staple for us. Not only on the trail, but year-round, we just can't live without our morning cup of 1,000 Mile Tea. As the Chinese proverb attributed to Lao Tze states, 'The journey of a thousand miles begins with a single step'... we now have a cup of tea to start us on our journey."

~ Marti Steury,
Executive Director – Alaska
Yukon Quest International, Ltd

"*This is a fantastic book about tea. Rather than from classical oriental perspectives as the most tea books do, the author elaborates this magnificent plant leaves originated from ancient and mysterious China tea plantation with a totally modern Western point of view.*"

这是一本非常引人入胜的关于茶叶的书籍，它通过不同于传统的来自于古老东方的视角，而是来自于现代的美国实际工薪阶层的视角，向大家介绍着来自于中国的，古老而神奇的东方树叶！茶！

~ Johnny New 牛张翼
Gengxiang Ninghong Tea Company

The Essence of Tea

The Transformational Journey of a Tea Connoisseur

By Jenny Tse

The Essence of Tea
The Transformational Journey of a Tea Connoisseur

Published by Sipping Streams Publishing
374 Old Chena Pump Rd.
Fairbanks, AK 99709

ISBN: 978-1-7329380-0-7

Cover design by Cathy Peluso
Cover photography by Whitney McLaren

these materials and information. Adherence to all applicable laws and regulations, both advertising and all other aspects of doing business in the United States or any other jurisdiction, is the sole responsibility of the purchaser or reader.

This book is intended to provide accurate information with regard to the subject matter covered. However, the Author and the Publisher accept no responsibility for inaccuracies or omissions, and the Author and Publisher specifically disclaim any liability, loss, or risk, whether personal, financial, or otherwise, that is incurred as a consequence, directly or indirectly, from the use and/or application of any of the contents of this book.

To my mother, father, and the Sipping Streams family. Without you, none of this would be possible. You are the ones who have shaped my life and challenged me to be a leader through all my struggles. Your stories, your experiences, and encouragement motivate me every day to continue the Sipping Streams mission. Thank you for all of your love and support throughout this tea journey.

Table of Contents

Foreword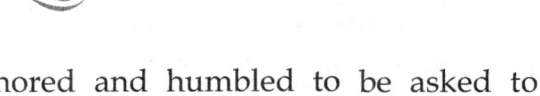

I am honored and humbled to be asked to write a foreword for such a book as this.

I met Jenny at several expos in Fairbanks, tasting different types of teas. We would talk and slowly get to know each other. I didn't purchase any teas right away because I became a coffee drinker after I moved to Alaska.

She notified me about a tea workshop she was going to teach online, so I signed up to learn more about loose leaf tea. I come from the South where we drink sweet tea, whether it's brewed on heat or sitting in the sun. I had no idea tea had so many benefits. I also didn't know that different types of teas require specific temperatures, steep times and can re-steep up to six times to get the best taste out of the leaves.

As I have gotten to know Jenny, I have found out how passionate she is about health and tea. She is hardworking, caring and patient. She also has an amazing spirit. All of these traits have led her journey to opening her own tea company in a place filled with coffee on almost every block. She shares her knowledge through her business, teaching online workshops, starting a tea university and now writing this book.

Most people don't go to school for health and education and end up somewhere unexpected. They stay where they are. Jenny allowed herself to follow this unknown journey. She stepped out of her secure comfort zone. Because of this, everyone around her benefits.

I love how her journey took her to China to personally learn how tea leaves are grown and harvested, especially how she was interested in the workers and working conditions.

Recently, I was told I cannot drink any type of coffee bean because it affects my health. I am grateful for Jenny teaching me what type of tea helps for different ailments and which have caffeine, especially on days when I need caffeine.

I believe in Jenny and all of her ventures. She pours her heart and soul into every aspect of what she does and is not afraid to work hard for it. I am proud to call her my friend and look forward to what comes next.

~ Nancy Ann Durham

Chapter 1

"Are You Drinking Tea Because You're Chinese?"

It's a question I get because, first of all, I look Chinese: "Are you drinking tea because you're Chinese?"

I hear that question and wonder, "What does that even mean? Drinking tea because I'm Chinese? What does it mean for tea to be Chinese? Am I Chinese? What does *that* mean?"

These questions that I've pondered have led me on an interesting journey that has, in part, led me to create my business and write this book.

When I started drinking tea, I honestly had no idea about the history of tea or what tea meant and represented. I forgave my college friends in Idaho for asking what seemed like a silly question to me: "Do you drink tea because you're Chinese?"

Actually at the time, I was only starting to drink tea. I wondered, "Doesn't everyone in the world drink tea?" I could understand that my being from Alaska, having been born in Hong Kong, and now attending college in a state that was not very culturally diverse would make that question come up. My friends probably didn't understand why I was drinking tea. I was a coffee drinker and have been drinking coffee since I was four. But in looking back, I guess tea is Chinese. Like I said, I forgave them.

As I began to think about that question and the bigger question – "What does it mean to be Chinese?" – more deeply, I realized that I didn't feel like I fit in and belonged anywhere culturally. I was born in Hong Kong as a first-generation American. I was the first in my family to graduate from high school and college, and I grew up in Alaska, which is far removed from the "Lower 48." Honestly, I didn't know who I was and how I fit into the world or even into my circle of friends. My Chinese family thought I was too white; my white friends thought I was still so Asian… and I just wanted to be *me*.

Me – the oldest child of Chinese parents who lived practically her whole life in Alaska. My father's family left China in the mid-1950s and settled in Hong Kong, later relocating to Alaska where my mother (also from Hong Kong) and I joined him when I was just over a month old.

Me – the coffee drinker turned tea drinker, the one who heard the question in college about tea and began to wonder about its origins and its meaning. So I researched.

Tea's History

When I delved further into the history of tea, I learned that all cultures around the world accept that tea *is* from China. I'd heard the colloquial phrase about "all the tea in China," meaning, of course, a lot!

The origin concept is unique because there are so many myths and legends about tea that are actually quite similar. Let's be clear: There is no dispute that tea is from China.

One of the myths about tea's origination is that the Emperor Shennong (also translated as "God Farmer" or "Agriculture God") traveled through the country and asked an aide to retrieve water from the river. The assistant did so and returned with hot water. It is a Chinese tradition to sanitize everything – cook everything, eat nothing raw or fresh to avoid possible food-borne illness. With this in mind, it makes complete sense that the aide returned with hot water – already sanitized and ready to drink.

According to the legend, the water the aide retrieved came from a stream into which a tea leaf had fallen. When the emperor sipped, he thought the water tasted absolutely amazing! He asked the aide to show him the place from which he'd gotten the water and, when returning to the spot, discovered the tea plant.

Another myth – a bit more gruesome – about the origin of tea involves the Buddhist monk, Bodhidharma who lived during the 5th or 6th century and whose teaching and practice centered on meditation. According to this legend, he was meditating at the wall of the Shaolin Temple and closed his eyes ever so slightly and accidentally dozed off. He was so ashamed of this that he immediately cut off his eyelids, so it would never happen again.

The goddess Guan Yin (which translates to the "Goddess of Mercy") took pity and mercy on him and grew tea leaves from his eyelids so Buddhist monks in deep meditation would remain awake as a result of the energy and caffeine provided by the tea leaves and tea.

To this day, you'll discover that many Buddhist monasteries have tea farms on their grounds, surrounding them.

More than Tea

In addition to learning about tea, I wanted to better understand and learn more of what it means to be Chinese. As I dove deeper into my tea journey, it became a very healing process. Many of my friends encouraged me to start a tea business, but that was not what I was trained to do. My college degrees, in education and health, weren't leading me in that direction. My interest in tea was continually stoked because people around me kept asking me questions about tea, not the least of which was, "Do you drink tea because you're Chinese?"

In order to more fully understand tea, a trip to China seemed to make sense, so I made my plans.

As I researched and planned my route through the country for my Chinese tea journey, my parents only asked the week prior to my departure about where exactly I would be going. Honestly, it had never occurred to me to tell my parents where I was going overseas because I was one to always do my own thing. Every member of my family is highly independent and never communicated too much about where we'd be going or what we'd be doing.

With their question about my destination, I realized that I should tell someone in my family what my itinerary was in case of some emergency. I'd arranged the trip on my own – highly focused and very excited about what I would get out of this "business trip." Although I hadn't yet launched, my business existed on paper as well as in my head.

I pointed to my destination on the map, and my mother's eyes grew wide with excitement. It was the very place my father had been born. Growing up, we did not discuss our family history. All I knew was that my parents came to America for a better life, and I always deeply respected and loved them for all they did for us. I had no idea where my father was born and never thought to ask. When my father overheard the conversation, he ran in to look at the map on the computer screen. As a serious man who typically doesn't show emotion or excitement, he looked at the monitor, looked at me, flared his nostrils, and walked away. I know my father well enough to know that when he flares his nostrils, he's very happy, excited, or thinks something's funny. He never comments on how someone (me included) should live their life or what they should do. But his flared nostrils indicated to me that he was very happy about my destination.

It was a serendipitous coincidence – and connection. I was now even more excited about my approaching journey.

At the time of my departure, I was one of two teachers in a small private school. While waiting to board the plane, I phoned one of the student's parents to ask if they'd deposit my paycheck since we didn't have direct deposit. I wanted to be sure to have funds available during the trip. I was simultaneously handing over my boarding pass and on the phone listening to the parent inform me that in the coming year, the school would be down to five students from 11. "You're not going to have a job when you come back." The news of my layoff literally hit as I was boarding the plane.

Disaster? Quite the opposite. I sat down in the plane seat and realized that for the first time, and possibly in my entire life, I had complete peace come over me. My only thought as I reveled in the peace washing over me was, "Wow. I guess I'm really doing this tea business. I'm on this plane without a really, really solid plan, but let's do this. Let's see where this leads."

I knew I'd need a translator and, once I landed, met a man who was there as a business consultant. I did not speak Mandarin Chinese. Yes, it seems so strange to be Chinese but not speak the language. It had been a struggle I had since childhood. As youngsters, my younger sister and I attended Chinese school, and we continuously felt like we didn't belong – we felt completely left out. All the other Chinese kids made fun of us because we didn't speak "Chinese." Untrue. We actually spoke Cantonese since our family was from Hong Kong. We simply didn't speak Mandarin – the language of mainland China and Taiwan. It added to a rough upbringing and certainly contributed to the sense of not fitting in: We didn't feel very white, being from a Chinese family, and at the same time, we didn't even feel Chinese being around other Chinese kids because of the language mismatch.

So my translator was a white man who'd lived and raised his family in China. Consider the seeming absurdity of the situation: A white man translating for a Chinese woman who did not speak a lick of the language while in China! The people I met also saw how ridiculous it looked. "Where are you from? Alaska? You really look Chinese. You are Chinese?…. I thought you said you were from Alaska…. Why don't you speak Mandarin?"

It perfectly underscored the conundrum that was my life and identity crisis.

Visiting Tea Farms

Landing in China felt completely surreal. I'd seen and remembered plenty of paintings of the landscapes of the country with mountains and misty clouds. My grandfather painted those scenes when I was a child. When I got off the plane, I felt like I was literally transported into that landscape scene. The paintings I recalled looked exactly like what I was now seeing in front of me.

I kept pinching myself. "Is this really real? Am I dreaming? Or am I really here? Those mountains can't be real. They look too much like the paintings." But it had to be real although it felt so much like a dream. Part of my reality was that I had just landed in a country without knowing anyone or even so much as a word of the language. But those mountains!

My visit to the first tea farm brought needed relief from the language challenge (and need for a translator) and that of being alone. I met a woman who was on a retreat at this tea farm for personal healing, much like me... and she spoke English! She was Chinese and had returned to China to come to terms with her personal history – to find closure and healing. She shared with me her very vulnerable story about her departure from the country decades earlier. She and her twin brother were in Beijing during the Tiananmen Square protests. That incident prompted her to leave China as she was horrified about the turn of events. Her brother remained in country, very disappointed about her decision to leave and refusal to agree with his nationalistic views.

When we met, it was her first time back in the country since that incident. Another serendipitous turn of events – the first person I met was returning to China to heal her family, her history, and her past... and so was I... both of us staying at a tea farm to gain clarity, awareness, space, and healing. I shared with her a bit about my own history and subsequent cultural identity crisis. It was obvious to me that our paths were destined to cross and that we were meant to meet each other. For me, that meeting was the start of my journey – both literally and figuratively.

Learning about Tea

It was exciting to see the tea leaves – the baby tea leaves, two leaves and a bud about which I'd always heard. It was amazing to also walk among these not-so-small tea bushes. Walking out onto the hillside where the bushes grew was very deceiving. I'd seen pictures and imagined them as small shrubs. In reality, they are very tall, trimmed trees.

The perspective reminded me of walking out into the tundra in Alaska. The tourists on the buses who travel through Denali National Park look out the windows and think, "Wow, look at all of those tiny shrubs and bushes." However, when they get off the bus and walk up to what they thought was a small shrub, they discover it is, in reality, a gigantic tree. In Alaska, the first thought about that changed perspective is, "There is no way I could see a bear behind one of these trees. It's huge and its trunk would easily hide it."

I initially felt that same anxiety walking among the tea fields, but my translator assured me quite confidently that there were no bears or wild animals to maul me around the tea bushes. Whew. Big relief.

My up-close-and-personal encounter with the tea bushes and perspective adjustment gave me great respect for the women who harvest the tea leaves. It is no easy task to pick these thick, leathery tea leaves – by hand, looking at them and only picking the best ones. These tea fields go on for miles and miles and miles. Yet somehow, everything is completely organized, every leaf is noticed, and everyone knows where every bush is. There is an ocean of tea leaves that go on seemingly forever, and it is all very nicely groomed. There is a lot of work in the tea industry along with a lot of passion and a lot of heart. It is definitely a labor of love.

I was impressed and amazed meeting the various harvesters and pickers at the tea fields. These people were not the owners but rather employees. These employees were well taken care of in their jobs. Free-range chickens walked throughout the tea fields that could be had for dinner. Children were provided education and school attendance was required. There were no children picking tea leaves. I presumed that might be a fair trade issue, but the old women picking tea laughed at that idea. "Why would we let children pick tea leaves? They would do a terrible job! They wouldn't know what to pick, and we don't want them to mess up our process."

I learned a lot through many of my very naïve questions.

The landscape was so clean, so refreshing, so far away from any city or smog. It was a pristine, simple paradise.

I went on to visit other tea farms and factories. Some were quite remote. One so remote that our vehicle couldn't go off-roading to get around gigantic boulders and other obstacles. We had to get out of the car and hike a few miles the rest of the way to reach the farm. As it turns out, this tends to be the rule rather than the exception. Most tea farms are nowhere near big cities… or even accessible roads!

In traveling to various farms, regardless of how remote or more easily accessible they might be, one theme emerged: Those who picked tea, harvested tea, or made tea were all very humble. Their message was typically, "This is what we have. Sorry it is not very beautiful, but it tastes amazing."

Honestly, with everything I'd learned, it was all amazing. It didn't matter what it looked like. I knew it was hand-harvested, hand-processed, and made with love and passion.

With the lessons I learned about tea while I was in China, it is still difficult for me to believe that tea is the number one consumed beverage in the world. So much work goes into the tea industry! The next time you go into Starbucks, take a close look at the menu. You'll likely see that tea is the cheapest drink you can get.

How can something be so inexpensive yet be so extraordinarily difficult and time-consuming to produce? That idea struck me as another conundrum along my journey.

Chapter 2

Starbucks® vs. Red Rose

So tea – quite expensive to produce yet so inexpensive to buy.

I started drinking tea because I was looking for a less caffeinated option as a hot beverage. Growing up, hot beverage consumption in my family was very common and included coffee, soup, hot water, and sometimes tea. It was actually uncommon for anyone in my family to simply drink a glass of water (unless it was hot). As a college student struggling to save money and not spend too much when joining my friends or studying at Starbucks, tea was the least expensive item on the menu. It became my choice. Less money on coffee, more money to save to start paying off student loans, especially as that deadline loomed as graduation was quickly approaching.

About the same time, a friend who had been diagnosed with leukemia and was leaving college left me with most of her pantry items. This included a gigantic box of Red Rose tea. I began drinking it just to stay hydrated. Still wanting to maintain the social aspect of Starbucks – hanging out with my friends or studying – tea became my regular menu choice because it would be rude not to buy *anything*... and tea was the cheapest thing I could buy.

My friends noticed my shift from coffee to tea and asked me about it. My degree was in athletic training, so they typically asked questions about health and nutrition and questioned if there was a particular health implication about drinking tea over coffee. They'd also heard information about the health benefits of tea, e.g., that it would cure cancer or similar and often unsupported claims. Here I was with extensive knowledge about nutrition… and I was drinking tea. Honestly, I was drinking tea because it was the cheapest thing on the menu.

In addition to being less expensive to purchase, I also knew that you could continue to add water and re-use the tea bag. However, I quickly noticed that these tea bags (and many others) would only yield about two cups of tea, so I'd have to buy another tea bag after that. Still far less expensive than a "quad venti soy inverted caramel macchiato at 140 degrees" that I'd been purchasing every day. That was $5.26, including sales tax, out of my pocket.

At home, I was drinking the Red Rose tea I'd inherited and also began trying Tazo® tea when I'd finally finished the box of Red Rose and was now buying tea at the grocery store. I really didn't know anything about tea other than it was a flavored beverage. I began noticing different brands of tea at the store, so I began experimenting and tasting different ones. Clearly, they were not all the same. Some came in the traditional, rectangular paper tea bags, some were in circular discs, and some were in transparent pyramid-shaped tea bags that I'd never seen before. At this point, I was neither a tea collector nor a connoisseur. When I ran out, I tried a different brand or type. I did not have cabinets full of tea. Time to restock? Tried a new flavor or brand. And a box still lasted a very long time.

My Tea Education

With my college education complete and me chipping away at student loans by choosing tea over that $5.26 macchiato every day, I took an online course about tea because, as an athletic trainer, I was still fielding numerous questions from co-workers about the health benefits of tea, perhaps others thinking I was setting some sort of example. "Do you know what different teas are? Are there different qualities of tea? How do you choose?"

The online course was pretty intense. Students had to taste tea every day and actually open tea bags to examine the contents. That exercise led to my discovery that not all teas are the same. In fact, my most horrifying realization about tea was that my favorite brand (that came in a circular paper disc and that I bought daily at my favorite coffee shop where I lived in Alaska) had one of the lowest grades of tea leaves. The instructor told us to rip open our favorite tea bags, look at the leaf particle size, and watch how the leaves unfurled in water… if they unfurled at all or remained as tiny white specs, essentially little pieces of dust. That's what I'd been drinking! Little pieces of dust.

Even worse, upon closer examination, you could see that the contents weren't even leaves. Sometimes there were bits of twigs or tiny pebbles. My experiment with this immediately led to, "Oh my gosh! My tea bags have tiny particles." I couldn't believe my eyes, so I ripped open a second tea bag with the same result. "No way. This can't be true!" Ripping open bag number three revealed more of the same. Shocked to discover my favorite tea was of such low quality. I ended the experiment and stopped ripping open tea bags, but a light bulb went on, and I now understood why I could not re-steep my favorite tea as often as possible with other teas.

The Real Cost of Tea

There's a lot more to the story about the cost of tea than my effort to save money by purchasing tea rather than a far more expensive coffee drink. High-quality teas can be re-steeped about four times, sometimes more. As the online course progressed, I learned that some steepings don't even achieve their full taste until the second or third steeping. My favorite, Ti Kwan Yin oolong tea (named for the mercy goddess), is one you can re-steep up to six times. And yes, it definitely tastes better about the fourth steeping.

It became clear that the tea from my favorite little coffee shop required two tea bags to even make one 20-ounce cup of tea. Ultimately, cheaper tea is not cheap at all. It obviously costs more because you have to use more tea… or at least more materials and tea bags than the actual tea leaves. Although higher quality teas may seem more expensive up front, in reality, the cup of tea they produce only costs about $.25 each.

Additionally, because of the leaf size in higher quality teas, they hold more nutritional value. These tea leaves are tightly rolled. Hence the reason that the best flavor only happens after a few steepings. The leaves need to unfurl. The nutritional value is boosted in much the same way that whole spices are better than ground spices. Ground spices lose more of their essential oils than their whole counterparts that you grind yourself. That said, you don't grind tea leaves; you simply let them unfurl slowly, so they transform the flavor, becoming more complex and stronger after the initial steepings. A ground tea leaf will lose all of its flavor after the first steeping. This is why an inexpensive tea won't provide much – if any – flavor after the first steeping. By the second or third steeping, you end up with tinted water but little else. You won't actually be getting a cup of tea.

Good tea is definitely worth it. Ultimately, good tea is a much better value, both for what you pay and for the flavor that hits your tongue.

Do Your Own Experimenting

Do what I did in my online course: rip open your favorite tea bag. Look at the tea particle size. Do they look like tiny pebbles? Do you see twigs in the mix? Place the tea leaves in a small cup of hot water and note how the tea leaves expand in volume. High-quality tea leaves are very tightly rolled. Once they absorb water, they expand a lot. These leaves always remind me of those foam sponge animal shapes that came packed in a capsule – put the capsule in water or in the bathtub and some animal shape would magically appear after a few minutes. (I loved these when I was a kid! As an adult, I've substituted the magic of the unfurling tea leaf.)

Various tea leaves absorbing water

Noticeable differences in various tea leaves

The larger the leaves are once they expand, the more often they can be reinfused versus the typical tea bag. So rip open your favorite tea bag to see exactly the grade and quality of the tea leaves it contains. You might find that you're as horrified as I was. Really, I'm drinking *that*?

I'm happy to share that the tea that was my favorite when I first ripped open the tea bag and found pebbles and twigs has started to sell a much higher quality of tea, including loose leaf teas. Today, I've found eight-foot displays for this tea in some stores with a very wide variety of teas of all qualities. There is still no doubt you will find what I did in the tea bags of some of the biggest names on the shelf. The point is that if you want to truly enjoy a good cup of tea, educate yourself. Find out what's in the bag.

Traditionally, there was a difference between the tea sold in tea bags and loose leaf teas, and in the past, loose leaf teas were superior. This goes back to the cost of production. Since there is expense that goes into the materials for a tea bag and the process of putting the leaves into the bag, tea bag companies (those with the square paper tea bags), put far less tea into the bag to offset the cost of materials and production and still be affordable.

One serving of tea should be 2.5 grams. Since traditional tea bag companies use a smaller particle size, it brews faster, so they tend to use about half the amount of a normal serving size. Most people don't notice the difference because they usually only have time for one cup of tea. You'll have a strong steeping of tea on the first use, and there is no real expectation that you'll use the tea bag for a second steeping.

With larger whole leaf teas, whether they're in a pyramid tea bag or loose in a canister, you'll typically use 2.5 grams. Keep in mind that these leaves are so tightly rolled that they are very dense – almost to the point that the leaf is vacuum-sealed on itself. This is how orthodox, high-quality tea leaves are produced and sold. Because the leaves are so tightly rolled, even in boiling water, the leaves take two to three minutes to *begin* to unroll, and all of the flavor doesn't come out at first.

This is the reason you can re-steep quality tea leaves several times. My favorite tea tastes best on the third, fourth, and fifth steepings. The first two are okay but certainly not as good as the later steepings. Someone who's new to tea might think the first steeping is fine; however, the flavor completely transforms *after* the second steeping. At first, that tiny tea leaf is about the size of a Grape Nut® cereal nugget, but with steepings, it will unfurl to an entire tea leaf that's been rolled 25 to 30 times. It is so compressed and dense that the hot water can't even penetrate the inner layers of the leaf to release its true flavor.

In my company, when we started to sell tea in the compostable pyramid tea bags, we used (and continue to use) the same leaves that we sell as loose leaf tea. We did not want to lower the quality to compromise for the convenience of using a tea bag. As a result, the compostable pyramid tea bags we sell are, in fact, more expensive than loose leaf tea. The reason tea bags at the grocery store seem inexpensive is because they've lowered the tea quality and quantity to offset the expense of packaging.

Not all teas are equal! Read the package to learn how much tea is actually in the tea bag, rip open one of the bags to see the tea leaves, put them in hot water and watch how they expand. A tea leaf's expandability in water is an indicator of the grade of tea. If you aren't sure, compare the leaf expansion from your tea bag leaves to higher quality leaves that you purchase as loose leaf tea.

Learning more about the various grades of tea is called "cupping." If you're interested, see the information at the end of this chapter to sign up for my online course.

Teaching Tea

I actually launched my company as a teaching platform – not to sell tea. As I'd mentioned earlier, I was a high school teacher, and after I took the online tea course, I was *really* enamored with tea. It seems I talked about tea all the time… drinking tea and then always talking about tea with friends and family. My students' parents noticed that I was knowledgeable about tea. It was hard not to. Anything I learn and am excited about, I then love to share.

The private school where I taught actually asked me to teach a semester-long elective course on tea so that I was teaching another elective in addition to physical education. "You know so much about tea, you should teach a class!" I already taught all the math, science, and other core curriculum classes. They wanted another elective course and thought tea was unique.

I designed the course for my students, and at the time, the idea of starting my own business was popping through my brain. As part of the course, I had my students design a website based on the information they'd learned about tea's history, health benefits, and brewing and steeping techniques. Our school was nonprofit, so we often held fundraisers throughout the year. It was fun for the students to apply what they learned, so we designed a tea workshop that we opened to the public to raise money. The students took turns teaching about the various aspects of tea. It was very well-received. We built on that success and expanded to a one-day workshop about tea, and also sold tea gift baskets and variety packs around the holidays. The students raised enough money to offset the cost of a trip to Seattle to visit different tea rooms and houses, so we could experience tea outside of Fairbanks, Alaska. At the time, there were zero tea rooms or tea houses in Fairbanks.

Fast forward to my China trip… with no job to which to return… I continued to build on my love of tea and teaching and began teaching classes in private homes (like Pampered Chef or any other home party experience). I knew I didn't want to sell tea. My focus was education. I wanted to sell classes. I started my company by dragging all of my tea pots, china, and kettles around in my truck to private homes for in-home tea demonstrations and classes, teaching about tea's history, health benefits, grades of tea, cupping, etc. As this evolved, customers wanted me to sell the product in addition to teaching about it, so I started buying and re-selling loose leaf teas and accessories.

As my company grew, it quickly reached "out-of-control" status as I was trying to work alone and work out of my small truck, constantly loading and unloading tea pots and supplies. Literally banking on the popularity of tea and the interest in learning about it, I opened a seasonal shop at Pioneer Park and hired a small team to help me. Pioneer Park is an historical theme park in Fairbanks that features original cabins from Fairbanks' gold rush era. We did this for one season and learned that the tourists weren't particularly interested in tea and what we offered, but the locals definitely were. The theme park only operated during the summer, and our building had no heat. No heat equals no building from September to May in Fairbanks, so I found a year-round store location at which my new team and I could offer classes, tea, food, and accessories. I also started blending my own teas.

At our Pioneer Park location.

Teaching about tea and running my own tea shop! It seemed great – the perfect business for me – and it was… for a while. Then the challenges hit.

Learn more about tea and cupping at: *http://bit.ly/learntea*

Chapter 3

"I Can't Do It All... But You Can!"

This was the phrase that I'd heard regularly from a friend at college. Let me take a moment to tell you a little bit about Tara. Tara had quite a lot of anxiety about accomplishing tasks and everyday living, from class projects and exams to simply talking with people on different topics to driving to church and having a car accident, worried about killing someone. Yes, that was a very extreme and unrealistic worry, but that was Tara.

Whatever I did, Tara's comment was always, "That's so amazing, Jenny. I can't do all that... but you can!" This was the ongoing theme of our friendship through five years of college – she couldn't, but I could. Tara was inspired to "be just like me because I could do everything." I did try to lead by example and shared that I also had struggles. I continually reiterated to Tara that I certainly wasn't doing everything perfectly, just trying my best.

To try to motivate her, I pointed out when Tara was accomplishing things and being successful – even about the things with which she was worried. "See Tara, you can drive. We're fine. We're in the car, going the speed limit, following the rules of the road... and our seat belts are fastened! Everything is fine." Despite my best efforts, I had trouble convincing her, and my encouragements were usually met with Tara's same old response, "I can't, but you can do everything, Jenny!"

This thought – and Tara's assessment of my abilities – was always in my head as I was wrapping up my college career. In reality, I was wondering what I was going to do next; where was I going? Back home to Alaska? It still seemed like "home" even though I'd been living in Idaho for quite a while. I was working to finish two sets of internships, driven by a double major in athletic training and physical education teaching. Athletic training required two years of internships, and in the final year, I had to complete student teaching to get my teaching certificate. It was overwhelming. I just tried to focus on the next task in front of me as Tara's words "I can't do it all… but you can" echoed through my brain every day.

It took a lot of energy, and I'd already cut back on my Starbucks order to save money and had also given up Mountain Dew. At first, I thought I'd experience caffeine withdrawals with these changes, but I didn't have the typical issues – no headaches, no caffeine cravings, no lethargy. Yes, I was drinking tea at the time since it became my money-saving beverage of choice – my trusty, inherited Red Rose tea.

Caffeine vs. Caffeine

Only years later, when I began studying tea, did I learn that tea has much, much more caffeine than coffee because of how the tea plant works. What's the difference? Is the caffeine in tea actually different than that in coffee? Perhaps you've heard that. That's another myth about tea. In reality, caffeine is caffeine. As a science teacher, I will tell you that the molecular structure of the caffeine found in tea and that found is coffee is identical. It is always the same. (If you're wondering, it's: $C_8H_{10}N_4O_2$.)

caffeine

However, how caffeine binds to different components in the tea plant is very different than how the process happens in coffee. The tea plant and leaf is very different than the coffee berry or pit, which we call the coffee "bean." When drinking tea, we're using the leafy part of the plant. The beverage comes from the leaves. On the other hand, the berry from which we get coffee as a beverage is not from the leafy part of that plant.

So why does tea seem like it has less or even no caffeine and why does it seem so relaxing to drink tea? It's simple. Tea has something coffee does not. Tea contains the amino acid L-theanine. This amino acid calms and relaxes your body. It exists in every single green leafy plant on earth. L-theanine actually exists in the coffee plant, but its presence is in the leaves, not the berry, and coffee doesn't come from the leaves. What we drink when drinking coffee comes from the berry, so the calming, relaxing component doesn't exist.

It makes so much sense to me in retrospect that I wasn't having caffeine withdrawal symptoms and the edginess that comes with them – I had not stopped consuming caffeine. With Mountain Dew, it's a sugar and caffeine rush, invariably followed by the crash. Coffee is similar since it doesn't come from the leafy part of the plant. Without L-theanine, there's no calming effect.

I didn't realize that I was consuming caffeine as a tea drinker. Perhaps I should have made the connection. There was constant study and project work that came with carrying 19 credits every semester. Plus I was working two part-time jobs, including my internship. Tea was actually helping me focus. The caffeine was keeping me alert and awake, and the L-theanine was simultaneously keeping me calm and relaxing my body. I was running on very little sleep every day without stressing out.

I took whatever came my way (tests, projects, etc.) one at a time. But Tara's voice was still in my head: "I can't do it all... but you can!" My thought: "What am I? Just a machine?" Once I spiraled into those downward thoughts, worry followed, so back to focus and concentration instead – being very disciplined to finish my last years of college.

Struggles Ensued

With college complete and my full-time teaching job now in the rearview mirror as the result of my layoff at the private school, it was a struggle to launch my business. I was supporting myself as a substitute teacher, and although that paid pretty well and provided me with flexibility, trying to balance every aspect of my life was challenging. I also got married around the same time, so there were plenty of changes and stressors in my life. Even "good" changes can be stressors.

The tea business started to blossom to the point that we opened a second location. Sounds good, right? As it turned out, we'd chosen to open in a mall that was beautiful, but there was not enough foot traffic and those who wandered in were pretty much the wrong demographic to buy. On the bright side, our lease for this location was month-to-month, so I was not faced with a long-term commitment, and this location was draining our profits. Our team was stretched thin between our permanent store location, the local fair and farmer's market, and now the mall store. It was clear the mall store had to go; however, that did not solve all of the other problems that had cropped up.

At the time I decided to close the mall shop, letters from the IRS started arriving. They were notifications about penalties and fees for failure to file my taxes correctly and on time. Multiple queries about this situation to my accountant were always answered with, "It was their mistake, and we'll take care of it." After repeatedly paying the fees for a few months (to avoid even greater escalation), it was obvious there was something very wrong – terribly wrong.

And at that same time, one employee failed to return to work. It turned out that she'd stolen all of our books and recordkeeping along with checks and a huge amount of cash. Because we'd become so diversified at so many locations, we hadn't made a deposit for a while. A friend of this employee came into the store and told us that this employee *had* stolen money because she actually bragged about it. This happened before I was even certain about it or could verify it. Her parents corroborated the story –

she'd also told them she'd done it without a speck of guilt or remorse. It was extremely an odd situation. And yes, it was also a very stressful situation.

So in addition to running the business, the other things on my plate now included a malpractice suit against my accountant, employee embezzlement, and a marriage that was falling apart. Tara's phrase that "You could do it all" could not have been further from the truth. It surely felt that it was not only impossible for me to do it all, getting through a single day was stressful.

The only thing I knew was to remain steady, keep the passion and core mission of the business in the forefront, and help my employees grow, providing stable employment for them. Both my employees and my customers needed me. I knew that tea helped me focus, so I continued to drink tea every day and take a few minutes – no matter what – to have a short "tea time." Despite feeling like I was being pulled apart and being pulled in every direction, tea helped me keep my focus.

All of these huge stressors hit at the same time, but surprisingly, I did not feel burned out and did not get sick. However, my employees had to remind me to eat and even brought nutritional drinks to work for me. "When's the last time you ate, Jenny? Are you eating today, Jenny?" They clearly knew the stress I was under. My tea drinking habit increased, and I drank that like a lot of people drink water. Tea drinking was not my focus; trying to hold everything together was.

Daily prayers were, "What in the world do I do, God? I can't do it all. If I'm meant to have this tea company, God – if this is what you really want me to do, then you need to put it together because I can't do it all." Like my friend, Tara, I said every day, "I can't do it all, God... but you can."

The result: Through the company, my staff and customers brought the healing I really needed during this very turbulent time. I wish I could tell you, as you're reading this book about tea, that getting through this was all because of the tea beverage, but honestly, God had a lot to do with it... all of it. God's presence in my life and the community of people He'd built around me and my tea company made a huge difference. And yes, drinking tea and the tea lifestyle did help a little bit, too.

The Science of Tea's Nutritional Value

So with God's help and the nutritional value of tea, I got through that very trying time without getting sick, even though incredible stress – and yeah, I was under incredible stress – often leads to illness, sometimes very serious illness.

As you'll recall, the tea beverage comes from the green, leafy part of the plant. Think about other green, leafy foods that are good for you – kale, spinach, broccoli, chard, etc. These are considered super foods, and yes, tea falls into that category. Tea is packed full of vitamins and nutrients:

- Vitamin C (immune system protection)
- Vitamin E (antioxidant)
- Vitamin K (skeletal health)
- Minerals, including fluoride
- Enzymes
- Methylxanthines

In addition to these very healthy ingredients, tea also contains polyphenols that are antioxidants. Antioxidants have the ability to combat cell damage. One of the most pronounced of tea's antioxidant properties comes from EGCG (epigallocatechin gallante). The importance of this particular antioxidant is that it is non-cell-specific. It does not favor one cell type in your body over another. EGCG "roams" throughout your body and when it binds to a particular cell, it places a "shield" around it. This shield protects the cell from damaging free radicals that might try to attach to it. Cells can be damaged by age, oxidative destruction, or possible mutation. Mutation is ultimately what leads to cancer. Damaged cells also lead to aging, premature and otherwise.

The great thing about EGCG is that it will protect any type of cell it finds – cardiovascular cells, smooth muscle cells, skeletal cells, blood and immune cells, integumentary system cells, nervous system cells… every single cell in your entire body. I can't stress enough how important EGCG's protective shield is, especially because of its non-cell-specific nature. It's a super defender in your body. And speaking of stress, when you're under a lot of stress, your body is in an imbalanced state and subject to producing more of those damaging free radicals. Knowing this, it's clear to me that tea was part of the reason I could go through a very stressful time without getting sick.

Additionally, one of tea's ingredients is methylxanthine, and it contains theophylline (helps improve respiratory function) and theobromine (a vasodilator that helps kidney and cardiac functions) as just two of its beneficial components. Together, they work to improve your systems, including your digestive system, helping to ensure that internal contractions and relaxations are occurring as they should. Instead of your body doing a sort of "internal hyperventilation" when you're under stress, the components of tea (especially in the methylxanthine group) are keeping your internal rhythms in check and functioning as they should.

There are countless studies done on the impact of tea on health and its ability to reduce many serious diseases. To read more about studies on tea at *Medical News Today*, visit:

https://www.medicalnewstoday.com/articles/269538.php

Matcha Madness

Matcha is a Japanese tea that is the most potent and technically the healthiest tea you can drink. It is now trending as a super food because of the way it acts in your body, although matcha has been around for hundreds of years. This type of green tea is specially grown and produced for the Japanese tea ceremony.

Matcha is "forced shade" grown, and in the spring, those who grow this tea place tarps over the tea fields to slowly starve the plant of sunlight. Plants that grow at higher elevations typically have naturally occurring cloud coverage that limits their exposure to sunlight, and the result is that the plants' ingredients are more potent. For example, Alaskan blueberries grow in very harsh, cold conditions in the tundra, so they are more potent and more packed with nutrients and antioxidants than their counterparts that are grown in the Lower 48. They're smaller, darker, and far more dense.

The same is true for a tea plant grown in harsh conditions or in forced shade. The plants will grow more slowly, but they'll be more densely packed with nutrients… and all the good stuff! This is why matcha is forced shade grown. Additionally, the Japanese dry the tea leaves using steam, so more of the plant's chlorophyll is intact. This is why Japanese green teas taste more "seaweed-y" or fishy than Chinese green teas that are heat dried. After the drying process, the stems and veins of the leaf are removed. It's also ground into one-half micron fine powder (finer than a smoke particle). As a result, with matcha, you're drinking more of the pure "meat" of the tea leaf than you would when drinking steeped high-quality loose leaf teas. Instead of steeping the leaf four or five times, you are drinking the all of the powerful ingredients of the leaf in one drink.

As you can see, matcha is a very, very potent green tea because of the way it's grown, produced, and consumed. If you want the most benefit and effectiveness from tea, this is the best option. I drink matcha when I am facing big deadlines. However, 100 percent of the caffeine is also in there, so it's not recommended to drink bowls and bowls of it. In the Japanese tea ceremony, matcha is prepared in bowls with a bamboo whisk. The bamboo fibers in the whisk are able to cling to those half-micron-size particles to achieve the desired frothiness. Using a wire whisk or a fork to mix your matcha results in lumpiness, so that is not recommended… unless you want to drink little lumps of potent tea balls.

If you want a lot of caffeine and 100 percent of all the beneficial nutrients of tea, matcha is the way to go. According to folk lore, matcha (and kombucha) were used to sober up the shōguns after they partied too late, so they could be ready for battle. (Whether or not you try it as a hangover cure is completely up to you.)

Learn more about "Matcha Madness" at: http://bit.ly/learntea

"I Can't Do It All... But You Can!"

Chapter 4

"... Like Your Parents"

Similar to my friend Tara's assessment and insistence that I "could do it all," I also faced many assumptions about my cooking skills: "You must be a good cook like your parents." Let's face it. We all live a bit in the shadow of other's success, giftedness, talents, and expectations.

When my parents immigrated to America, they were cooks. My father left home when he was 13, joined the merchant marines and became an apprentice chef, traveling and cooking around the world. Obviously, he began cooking at a very young age. Growing up, I didn't realize the great cooking skills that both my parents had. They both worked at what was, at the time, probably the only Chinese restaurant in Fairbanks, working there until of the end of the Alaskan pipeline boom. When that restaurant closed, my parents opened their own restaurant.

As a result, my parents gained a reputation as very, very good chefs in Fairbanks. When my parents lost the restaurant due to a bad partnership, my father then became a consultant and was ultimately the force behind many restaurants that opened in the area. He knew food and he knew how to cook. Many people even asked my parents to cook for them or to teach them how to cook. Because of my parents' skills in the kitchen, everyone who knew our family assumed that I was as good a cook as they were... and still are. Nothing could be further from the truth.

First, since both parents were so good in their profession, they didn't have much time to teach the kids to cook. In addition to lacking time, my father also lacked patience to teach me to cook. As kids growing up, my siblings and I did not do many of the typical household chores because my father could do things better and faster, so he did. We didn't even mow the lawn because, as kids, we couldn't do it perfectly, and he wanted a perfect lawn. Perhaps this is a cultural trait. I'd learned on my trek through China that children did not pick tea leaves because they couldn't do it perfectly.

The result? Growing up, I did no cooking at all. I recall one summer, my mother gave me a baking book from Carrs Foodland (a grocery chain that first launched out of Anchorage and spread throughout Alaska). Since there seemed to be nothing to do during the summer – we did not have cable TV – and my sister and I wanted to stay busy, I decided to bake every recipe in the book. Every day, my mother returned home to scads of cookies and cupcakes! The Chinese culture does not gravitate toward sweets and pastries. Dessert consists of fruit instead. When my mother wondered what I would do with everything I baked, I told her I'd give it all away.

Of course, my mom wasn't very pleased that I was baking every day and then giving it all away – cookies, brownies, cakes, cupcakes... everything! I couldn't understand her aggravation about it. After all, she bought me the book. Why wouldn't I use it? In fact, that summer, I won every baking contest division that I entered in the state fair and did earn my own spending money for the fair. Plus, I had plenty of ribbons to display.

Baking and cooking, however, are two completely different things. You can be a great baker but a lousy chef, just as I had proved. On the other hand, my mom was a great chef but wasn't the mom who baked the way my friends' moms did. After his restaurant consultancy business, my father worked for the Alaska pipeline as a chef, flying from pump station to pump station. He'd be gone for a month at a time, and when he returned home, he'd park a big toolbox in the garage. It was the same type of toolbox a carpenter or mechanic might have... only I didn't understand why he would have a tool box if he was a chef. To my surprise, when my father opened his tool box, it was filled with cooking and baking tools and implements rather than wrenches, screwdrivers, and hammers. He also had a metal-clad, very industrial-looking recipe book along with his two huge toolboxes. These toolboxes and book looked exactly like they should for someone working on the pipeline.

Alaskans know that the pipeline workers ate very well. And employees could drive a hard bargain when it came to their desire for good food. Before my father worked for the pipeline, there was a famous milk strike. When workers didn't get the milk they wanted, they refused to continue working on the pipeline. When my father was at home for his two weeks off between stints on the pipeline, he'd practice and hone his baking skills, including baking doughnuts from scratch, biscuits, quiches, etc. We ended up with a kitchen full of American food to which we were very unaccustomed. He was the one who could both cook and bake very well.

Defying Expectations

When I launched my business and opened my tea house, there were plenty of expectations about it. My parents' friends would stop in to check it out and expected that the food would be as good as that which my parents prepared. "Your food must be as good as your parents. You must be a good cook like your parents." Wrong. And I knew that.

The menu was very simple. We made homemade steam buns, a Chinese staple, when I was growing up. I'd helped my mom make those for the farmer's market when I was a child, so I knew how to make them and knew I wanted them on the tea house menu. I also knew the food menu had to be modest, and that was based on my parents' advice: "Never open your own restaurant! Whatever you do, don't go into the restaurant business."

I took their advice to heart – a little – when I opened the tea house. After all, it was not the full-fledged, full-service restaurant like my parents had when I was growing up. The tea house was (and is) much more like a café with small treats and very simple food items. After all, the tea is the focus.

However, I ignored their advice not to start my own business. They were disappointed when I opened my business. Being from an immigrant family, going to high school and graduating from college with two degrees, my parents wanted the most stable future possible for me. Owning a business is not without risk and can certainly be unstable. In the beginning, my parents were very hesitant to be enthusiastic about my venture. In fact, they were not very supportive at all. They figured it would be a phase that I went through, having some fun, but ultimately snapping back to reality and finding employment in a school district or health care facility where I could put my formal education and training to work.

Creating Success

After my second year in business, I was featured in the *Tea Almanac*. Each year, three international tea companies are featured. I'd won second place in the North American Tea Championship with our Alaskan Fireweed and Low Bush Cranberry White Tea blend. This was the first time I'd entered tea into an international competition, so I created a blend that reflected me and that also reflected Alaska. My mother helped me harvest hundreds of wild Alaskan fireweed flowers. We also loved picking berries, so I added cranberries to the blend. Although this was one of several entries, I was shocked that one of our hand-harvested ingredients that we dried like traditional Chinese tea leaves won in international competition.

This led to the *Tea Almanac* contacting me to do a story. At the time, I didn't take it too seriously and thought it was a joke because I didn't really know what the publication was or its caliber in the international industry. When I was sent a copy of the magazine that contained my story, I recognized it and recalled seeing it in specialty tea shops and at coffee and tea conferences. It was hard to believe my own photograph was in this very well-known publication! I immediately went to my parents and found my father relaxing in bed. I showed him the article on my laptop: "Look Dad, I'm featured in an international magazine!" When he realized the magnitude of what I was showing him and the importance of my accomplishment, he did his nostril flare, and then I quickly left the room. I had gotten my moment of approval from him, and it was all I needed.

Since then, we've won 11 international awards for the teas we source, blends of tea, and making tea, including receiving first place at the World Tea Expo competition for the Top Tea Infusionist – a competition for preparing and serving the perfect cup of tea (similar to an international barista competition).

Tasting Tea

While I'm not a good cook like my parents, my palate has been expansively developed probably as a result of genetics coupled with my upbringing that focused on amazing food. I know what good tea tastes like.

So how do you taste tea? Perhaps you have an image of sipping from a china cup with pinky raised. This might be true in some cultures. However, *tasting* tea professionally is quite different than how you might simply *enjoy* tea. Professionally tasting tea is enjoyable, but it is a learned skill and takes time. Your tongue has different zones, and taste buds are not evenly spread out. Anyone who does wine, chocolate, or cheese tasting knows that to taste something fully, you must taste it across and throughout your entire palate.

Since tea is a very hot beverage, trying to taste it across your entire palate can be, well, not so enjoyable until you learn how. There is a lot of tongue burning that occurs until you learn to properly slurp tea and spray it across your tongue. When I started, I mostly burned my tongue. It is very hard to slurp a beverage that is at 200 degrees and not burn your tongue.

With proper slurping, you will also pull in air through your mouth, spraying it over your whole tongue, and the air works to simultaneously cool the tea in your mouth. When most people learn to properly taste tea, they think it is very rude to slurp. Slurp? No way. Too rude. However, you must slurp to get the true taste of the tea. Unless you can taste the tea across your entire tongue and with all of the taste bud zones, you won't get the true flavor. Unless you slurp, a burned tongue and seared taste buds will result. Definitely not enjoyable. Definitely contradicts the image of the delicate, pinky up sipping.

Whenever people try anything new – from new food or tea – that is completely unfamiliar, there is often hesitation. In fact, they might not like it because they have no association with it. There is no point of reference. There tends to be a link between unfamiliarity and dislike. Unless there is a relationship to something they've tasted that is similar, they may equate the new taste with dislike. It takes about 20 tastes before you will develop a palate for something new.

We make many tea blends and tisanes (herbal infusions that do not contain tea leaves) that I personally do not prefer. In some ways, I would say I don't "like" them; however, I've developed a palate to design and create flavors for customers rather than myself. The term should always be "do not prefer," rather than "do not like."

For the full tea tasting experience like a professional, smell the dry leaves, look at the leaf shape, notice the details of how the leaves unfurl when infused in hot water, look at the color of the liqueur, smell the liqueur, taste the liqueur, look at its viscosity, and note the feel of it in your mouth. Hold the liqueur in your mouth, move it around your tongue, and push it to the roof of your mouth. It is very similar to wine tasting. In the industry, we use very similar, if not identical, terminology for tasting teas that the wine industry uses.

In tea competitions in which you are making the perfect cup of tea, there are also many, many similarities to wine making and tasting. The shape of the cup affects the way you experience tea in the same way that the shape of a wine glass affects its taste and your experience. The olfactory experience ultimately affects your sense of taste. The approach you use for wine tasting should be the same approach you use to taste tea. Except maybe the slurping! They're simply different beverages served at different temperatures.

As with tasting wine or even beer, temperature affects the taste of tea as well. A tea that is very hot will react differently with your taste buds than one that is served at a lower temperature. So hot, room temperature, and iced tea will all taste very different, even when produced from the exact same leaf or blend. Imagine very cold iced tea and think of having an ice cube on your tongue. To some extent, you are numbing your tongue. A very cold iced tea has the same effect – a little bit of numbing the taste buds. The result is that most people like iced teas that are very strong to counteract the effect of the temperature on the tongue and in the mouth. Cold is an excellent numbing agent – think ice pack on an injury. It can also numb your taste buds. They won't react the same, and the result is simply a different taste.

Different teas have different temperatures and steeping times at which they will deliver their true flavor. The hotter the water, the faster the extraction rate of the leaf's flavor. Some of the *typical* temperatures and steeping times for a single serving are:

- Green tea: 175 degrees F, 1-3 minutes
- Oolong tea: 195 degrees F, 3 minutes
- Black and herbal tea: 205 degrees F, 3-5 minutes

At a glance, you get a sense of how temperature and time affects taste! Using too much tea or using a different temperature and steeping time leads to a completely different result.

Your Experience

Taste is incredibly and completely subjective. You will develop your own palate from your own experiences and associations. There is no right or wrong way to express the way you experience tea and how it tastes to you. Like I said, it is entirely subjective. The same is true with anything you taste – it's you tasting it, no one else.

When I first started to learn to taste tea, I described it as memories I had based on what I knew about my grandfather and what he drank or the way he smelled. Smell is a very powerful memory trigger.

Some teas reminded me of the smell of his pillow or clothing. I did not have enough experience or the vocabulary yet to describe it any other way. While it was very pleasant, my description might be of walking through a cold, wet rainforest in Sitka, Alaska. That may not sound appetizing to someone else, but it was the triggered memory of the taste that might be described as musty and woodsy.

Learning how to express yourself – whether from something you lived through, smelled, or ate – is completely okay. It is your own personal experience and association. It is how you build and develop your palate for tea… or anything.

I encourage you to break out of your own mold of the assumptions you may have. You might just surprise yourself! A lot of people hesitate to drink teas they *assume* they don't like. We offer a "tea of the day" sample. On days when it happens to be a green tea, we often hear, "Nope. I don't like green tea." Based on their previous experience, they assume they don't like green tea. However, the offer is one sample of only one of our green teas… and we have eight different types. They all taste drastically different from each other.

Additionally, most people burn their green tea. Green tea should use only steaming hot water. As we just covered, temperature affects taste. If you steep delicate green tea in boiling water, you are going to have an extremely astringent, potent tea. This is probably what leads to "Nope. I don't like green tea." There's nothing wrong with it, but steeping at a high temperature forces the flavor too quickly. You now have a concentrated cup of tea. If you taste a green tea you don't prefer, add water and see what happens. You might find you enjoy it more by diluting it.

If there's a tea that you smell and don't think you'll like, be sure to make it the proper way before you pass judgment. Keep in mind also that it typically takes 20 tastings until you may develop a palate for it. You may never prefer it, but if you want to expand your palate, keep tasting. I encourage you to break out of your mold and habit of what you think you like and try many different teas!

At Sipping Streams Tea Company, we offer a wide variety of teas for sale.

Visit: www.sippingstreams.com and discover a new tea or one of your existing favorites!

"... Like Your Parents"

Chapter 5

"I Heard Tea Cures Cancer"

"Tea cures cancer." This was another comment I'd heard from a friend during college. In my science-based course of study as an athletic training student, my professors taught us to question everything! "Always research the science... but remember, things change, and in five years, you'll find another case study that proves otherwise."

I was hesitant to believe anything would or could act as a cure to cancer, and I had not read any research that would lead to that conclusion. Tea certainly has plenty of health benefits, but there is no proof that it cures cancer... or any other disease for that matter.

In studying and doing the required homework and research for athletic training, I read the *American Journal of Medicine* and other publications, and I did uncover case studies regarding tea's impact on health. Part of researching those case studies included understanding the demographics, the subjects in the study or experiment, how the research was conducted, the study duration, and whether there seemed to be any sort of bias.

Instead of claiming that tea had miraculous health benefits or that it cured anything, I shared with my friends what I'd learned – and what the science proved – about tea and its effect on the subjects in any given case study. In continuing to pursue my degree in athletic training, I continued to uncover more and more case studies about tea and saw that there was some benefit to it, but I was still very hesitant to believe the latent claims that tea could cure anything, especially cancer.

During this time, I dated a guy who had ulcerative colitis (UC) – an inflammatory bowel disease that causes long-lasting inflammation and ulcers in the digestive track. Because of his disease, he researched a lot to learn how different foods worked in the digestive system, and he also drank a lot of tea. His UC was pretty severe and had a really negative effect on his life, to the point that he had to drop classes and even had to drop out completely a few times because of this illness. It was very debilitating. His interest in the health benefits of tea was extremely personal, and he'd ask me many questions about what I'd researched and learned during my course of study.

In my post-college studies about tea, I learned more about EGCG and how powerful that antioxidant is. Cardiologist, Dr. Ronald Sebold offered a seminar on the health benefits of tea at the World Tea Expo during which he explained the physiology of antioxidants and how they worked in the body, including their strong anti-cancer impact and other health benefits that also included their beneficial impact on the circulatory system.

As I sat in the front row of this seminar, I was the only one without a glazed looked in their eyes. Quite the opposite. I was eating up every word with a big grin on my face. With my background in sports medicine, I was very familiar with the terminology regarding physiology and anatomy. It was very exciting for me. When I turned around to look at the rest of the attendees, they obviously had no idea what he was talking about and looked completely lost. They were struggling to understand and relate to the terminology he used.

Dr. Sebold completely focused on the science, just as I had been taught to do, and with his medical specialty, he focused on tea's impact on heart health as well as cellular repair. He also covered tea's impact on cholesterol and its adhesion to the artery walls, based on his own studies. Tea does not reduce cholesterol as some people believe. Instead, tea makes the plaque that results from cholesterol less binding, so it is less likely to cling to artery walls. The plaque buildup in arteries is what leads to the problems associated with heart disease and associated afflictions. Do not expect your cholesterol count to be lower because you drink tea. However, tea will help reduce the negative effects and artery clogging that result from having too much cholesterol.

Rooibos

Rooibos is a very powerful plant that is not tea, although many people refer to it as "rooibos tea." It is only grown in South Africa, and only within the last 20 years did it become a cultivated plant. Prior to that, it grew wild and was wild-harvested. All of the rooibos in the world comes from South Africa.

Rooibos has similar antioxidants to tea and some that are even more powerful than those found in the Camillia sinensis species – the plant that is tea that comes from the Theaceae family of plants. Rooibos (Aspalathus linearis) comes from the Fabaceae family that contains legumes; however, people drink rooibos like a tea. This evolved from the British tradition of having tea time during British rule in South Africa. As a result, rooibos has a reputation as a tea, and many people drink it with milk and sugar as they would tea.

It's not my place to correct tradition, but it is a completely different plant than anything found in the Camillia genus. It acts very differently in the body. One of the huge benefits of rooibos that people in South Africa have known for a very long time is that it is caffeine-free and is a very strong anti-inflammatory. Employing my learned "question everything" approach, I began to research case studies about rooibos. There was one study conducted on mice in Japan that showed significant correlation between rooibos consumption and decreased brain aging. There are countless other anecdotal accounts that it helps with food and seasonal allergies as well as skin or topical allergies. In fact, it will reduce inflammation on contact.

In Alaska, we joke that the mosquito is the Alaskan state bird. There are over 100 species of mosquitos in Alaska, and they can get quite large. When I worked at the airport during college summer breaks, I greeted one tourist getting off a plane with the usual, "Welcome to Alaska. What brings you here?"

"The mosquitos," he jokingly replied, but he went on to explain that he was an entomologist and was returning from Barrow (now known officially as Utqiagvik) in the far north where he'd been studying mosquitos – the perfect outdoor laboratory for his work.

Once I learned about the powerful anti-inflammatory properties of rooibos, I began using it as a topical application on mosquito bites and even a bee sting. It immediately provided pain and inflammation relief. I've had canker sores throughout my life, and when I would drink rooibos, it numbed them immediately. As a child, I often had canker sores and am not sure if they were caused by stress or diet. Chinese philosophy contends that there must be a dietary balance between hot and cold, the yin and yang. My mother insisted I ate way too many nuts and seeds, creating an imbalance that led to the canker sores. I used myself as a test subject for rooibos' beneficial properties and discovered that I didn't have to use Benadryl for mosquito and insect bites and could skip the yucky-tasting Anbesol® for canker sores. The results were fantastic.

Medicinal Properties

Last year, we had about five different customers tell us that they were drinking rooibos because it helped with their UC flare-ups. One of my regular customers, Lori Packee, told me that when she drank our African Sunset blend (rooibos and chamomile), she would have instant results from her own UC flare-ups. When Lori felt a flare-up coming on, the African Sunset blend would stop the symptoms.

Ulcerative colitis is a chronic autoimmune disease, and the accompanying inflammation can be very painful. Essentially, with UC, your own immune system attacks your colon, creating large ulcers in your lower intestine. It is a disease that, depending on the severity, can be very debilitating with difficult-to-manage symptoms. It is very much like a stomach ulcer with more consistent – almost constant – pain. Flare-ups can easily be triggered by stress and/or diet. Those who suffer from UC will tell you that they will try anything that might help ease the pain and allow them to live a more normal, everyday life.

Lori, along with other customers, confirmed that they were regular drinkers of the African Sunset blend because of the relief it provided from their UC symptoms.

This blend is the only one I've ever created specifically for medicinal properties. When I first started Sipping Streams Tea Company, people heard that I blended teas and was a tea specialist. That caused some to assume I was an herbalist. Nope. I'm not an herbalist and am certainly not a doctor. Yes, I have a background in athletic training and nutrition and the pharmacology understanding that goes with that. People came to me to ask for blends that might help with their various ailments.

One customer came into the store and told me she was having quite a number of digestive issues. "I heard you can blend teas. Can you make something for me?" I asked her several questions to better understand her symptoms and what might be going on in her body. Again, I'm not a doctor and would never take it upon myself to try to diagnose anyone! All I knew was what teas and ingredients I had and what I'd heard they could do along with a sports medicine background. After several questions, I learned that she was under a lot of stress and had a great deal of anxiety. She wasn't sleeping very well and was also having digestive issues along with pain. I certainly didn't want to ask too many personal questions... just enough to understand a bit more about what might be going on with her and what might be triggering her upset stomach.

I took two ingredients that I knew what they did – chamomile for its relaxing properties and rooibos for its anti-inflammatory properties – and blended them to create what we now call African Sunset. I gave her the blend and told her to drink it three times a day for a week, and then tell me how it worked for her. She was thankful at the prospect of getting relief, and I didn't charge her because I wasn't sure it would even work. "Honestly, I don't know if this will work for you. I just happen to know what these two ingredients do. If it turns out that it helps, come back and I'll blend more for you."

A week later, she walked in and exclaimed, "Wow! It tasted great and is so amazing. It totally worked. I want a pound of it!"

I explained that a pound would yield 160 fresh cups – quite a lot for an herbal blend and a lot to buy at one time. She would not be dissuaded. It tasted great, offered amazing results, totally worked, and she wanted a pound. So I blended her pound, and she went happily on her way.

About a month later, another woman came into the tea house with the exact story that I'd heard from the first woman – digestive issues, etc. I asked her, "Did the other lady tell you to come here?"

"What lady?"

No, she had not been referred. I explained that another woman had been in the month before with a very, very similar story and shared that I'd given her a blend that she swore helped alleviate her symptoms. I went to the back of the store and grabbed the leftovers from the previous batch. I explained that this was leftover and gave her the same directions: "Drink it three times a day for a week and let me know how it works."

Again, she was thankful and asked the price. Once again, I did not charge her because I wasn't certain it would work for her even though it seemed to work for the first customer. A week later, once again I heard, "It tastes amazing. It totally works. I want a pound of it!"

Not long after, we held a tea tasting and art exhibit at the tea house, and we decided to get rid of the leftovers from the last batch I'd blended. I didn't know when we might use it again, so we gave it away as free samples. I was unprepared for its popularity. Everyone who tasted it agreed that it was delicious, and their next question was, "Where can we find it on the shelf?" Gulp. I had to confess and apologize to everyone that the sample was from leftovers from a blend with which I'd simply experimented and wasn't planning to sell. Everyone recommended that I should sell it, and our African Sunset blend became a regular offering and is now one of our most popular chamomile blends.

As with any high-quality ingredients, you receive greater potency of the medicinal properties. Everything has a health impact – either helpful or harmful. The quality of the ingredients determines how potent or effective the medicinal properties might be.

Tisanes

As I mentioned, tisanes are herbal infusions rather than true teas. Different tisanes have different health benefits. They are not from the Camillia sinensis plant. The African Sunset blend that I mentioned is a tisane. There is no tea in it at all.

Out of everything we offer, our Midnight Sun herbal blend is our most popular and our number one best seller… and that includes all of the teas we offer as well. This tisane contains orange peel, lemon peel, hibiscus, rose petals, and rose hips. It is a very fruity and tangy herbal infusion that is very high in vitamin C and is caffeine-free. It's a great choice for people to enjoy as a nice treat before bed. Since Alaska is the land of the midnight sun, we named this tisane accordingly, and when brewed, it's beautiful and looks like a sunset with its reds and pinks. Although in Alaska in the summer, the sun really never sets! Technically, there might only be 23 hours of daylight with the sun actually dipping below the horizon for a brief time, but I assure you, it is still light outside.

The Midnight Sun herbal blend is one that we highly recommend for those who want and need a boost of vitamin C. Additionally, one of the ingredients, hibiscus, is very powerful in helping to regulate blood sugar and blood pressure. Because of the medicinal properties of hibiscus, the radiology department at the hospital in Fairbanks actually buys hibiscus from our shop for their patients. Many people get nervous to be scanned, so the radiology staff makes a cup of hibiscus for those patients to help regulate their blood pressure before the procedure.

It's important to remember that different plants will always have different medicinal properties. If you happen to have a certain condition for which you are taking medication, it's very important to always know what medicinal properties may be in what you consume. For example, if you happen to take Warfarin (sold under the brand name Coumadin) for its blood-thinning effect, your doctor may recommend that you drink tea. However, since people use "tea" a bit generically (i.e., anything infused in hot water is called "tea") and may include tisanes, that can lead to problems.

You must carefully check the ingredients in any herbal infusions that you drink, especially when you are taking medications. Ingredients in your herbal tea may be contraindicated for your medical condition and they may react with or counteract other medication you're taking. For example, some cancer patients may be taking a blood thinner or thickener. While chamomile has some relaxing properties, it is also a natural blood thinner, so drinking chamomile can either negate or exacerbate what should really be happening in your body.

Lifestyle Impact

No matter how many supplements you take for pure medicinal value or the quality of their ingredients, that alone will not guarantee good or even improved health. Think about the couch potato who might take something that is supposed to improve cardiac function but never considers even so much as taking a walk for exercise. Lifestyle matters.

The first case study I ever read in a professional medical journal was about Scandinavian men who drank tea. In this research, I realized that drinking tea is more than medicine and does more than provide a health benefit. It is a way of life and a way of being. The positive impact on the subjects in this study could be attributed to *lifestyle* in combination with the tea they were drinking. People who choose to drink tea have a certain rhythm in life because tea takes time. You have to wait for the water to heat and then wait for the tea to steep. You might also have to wait for the tea to then cool a bit. Yes, tea takes time.

In the history and culture of tea, there is a certain slow pace. To fully appreciate it, you have to slow down in what is otherwise a very fast-paced world. Certainly there are plenty of instant teas and ready-to-drink teas available, and those will provide some of the health benefits of tea. However, the combination of the medicinal properties and the lifestyle that surrounds tea drinking (at least a few minutes each day or longer for "tea time") is what boosts longevity. A balanced lifestyle impacts a person's overall well-being. Ingredients alone won't do it.

My grandfather took time to make tea every morning after his walk and tai chi exercises. He even did a Chinese tea ceremony every morning as well. It was all very slow, and his routine took a good bit of time every single day. As a child, I had trouble appreciating, or even understanding, it. I wanted everything fast and quick. "Why does Grandpa do his weird thing and take all this time out of his day?"

Now that I'm older and living in our fast-paced, instant world with social media and round-the-clock instant news everywhere, I realize that I have a need for calm. I have to sit down and make time and space for myself. I now realize my grandfather had it right all along. It makes sense for people who drink tea to probably have lower mortality rates because they're slowing down rather than speeding through their day... even if it's only for their own personal tea time. However, that tea time creates a mindfulness that tends to carry over into other parts of their day and lives. They're likely living more holistically and not simply eating and drinking certain things for their health benefits. It all fits together.

Certainly, you can buy a number of different teas and tisanes from Sipping Streams Tea Company, but if you want to experience the full benefits that tea provides, we offer the "Essence of Tea" course to help you more fully appreciate tea. Visit the "Universi-Tea" section of our website:

http://bit.ly/learntea

Chapter 6

Communi-Tea

There is definitely a certain lifestyle that surrounds tea and tea drinking. In fact, that is one of the reasons I started my tea company. I noticed that many people shared stories about their own experiences with tea with their families, friends, and loved ones. They talked about how tea brought comfort to them when they were sick or didn't feel well. They talked about how much they enjoyed taking time for tea as a break from daily activities. I realized that everyone I spoke with had some sort of memory or story tied to tea in their lives.

After all, tea is the number one most consumed beverage in the world next to water. However, tea isn't as popular in American culture as it is almost every place else around the globe.

The more I heard stories from people about tea and the time they spent with their families discussing it, the more I realized it was having an impact on my own life and family. As I shared both the information I was learning about tea and the beverage itself with my family, the more our own communications began to open up. That communication brought a lot of healing to my family.

The first tea farms I visited during my trip to China were in the very place my father was born, creating a wonderful connection for us, and tea also created a connection between my grandfather and me. As we drank tea together and discussed it, my parents and grandparents also opened up about their childhoods and shared stories they had that I'd never heard before.

Until that point, my parents remained quiet about the pain, struggles, and heartaches that they endured when they were growing up. As adults, they wanted a big change for their children – my siblings and me – when they moved to America. They didn't want the same struggles for us. When we'd ask questions as kids about their childhoods, they always avoided the questions and changed the subject.

I shared more with my family around the dinner table about what I learned about tea, the cultural aspects surrounding it, and its history along with the taste of tea and the different varieties and where they were grown. (Always a teacher at heart!) And a funny thing happened: my family started to talk to each other more. Now most American families do talk around the dinner table, but my family was a little bit different. During our mealtimes together, my sister and I would usually start arguing. This upset my father, and he would declare, "No more talking!"

The result was a few more bites in silence, and then we'd all move to finish dinner in front of the TV. For the most part, our meals were silent. We might start to have a conversation but a petty argument typically ensued, always followed by my father's insistence on silence. That was followed by eating in front of the television, watching *Wheel of Fortune*.

Tea as a Healing Medium

Besides the health benefits of tea on the body, tea was also bringing a lot of emotional healing to me personally and to my family. We didn't verbalize "I love you" as much as other people and other families did. We didn't give hugs the way I'd seen my friends share with their own families. Nor did my parents share about their personal lives the way my friends' families did.

In my family, we certainly didn't hate each other nor were we anti-social. Our version of fun and spending time with each other was either watching TV or fishing and camping. Being in Alaska, outdoor activities often happened in the rain. We were very competitive and always wanted to get our limit of halibut or salmon or whatever we happened to be fishing for. The whole family would spend time in a small tent – one made for three people when there were five of us. And we'd fish in the pouring rain all day. This probably doesn't sound like fun to you, but those are the fond memories of my childhood because it was when we spent the most time together as a family – driving together in the car for eight hours to fish in the cold and the rain.

Other fun projects for my family (that I realize now aren't fun for most) included working on the house. My father would say, "Here's a fun project for you, Jenny. Strip the paint off the whole house and repaint it." Actually, I never thought twice about this and didn't view it as work. I'd simply ask for directions about how to do it, and I'd get to it. My sister was the same way; however, when friends would visit, my father would forget that our friends didn't see this as anything but work. He'd give them tools and try to convince them to help. Then he'd leave us. We were treated to McDonald's or something similar at the end of a day of hard work. Of course, my friends didn't have this type of relationship with their own families and for them, "work" wasn't at all fun. They weren't work-aholics like my family tended to be – my family that did not verbally communicate the way theirs did.

When communication about tea opened up in my family, I thought, "Wow. What a powerful medium tea has been." Tea truly helped bridge a gap in my family and helped us become more intimate. Conversations that began about tea broadened and began to include memories and feelings as well.

If tea could bring healing and communication to my family that didn't socialize with each other a lot, I wondered what it could do for other people in addition to the health benefits it provided. How might it work to heal other people's personal relationships?

Tea Time

In the Chinese culture, there is a traditional tea time. Being from Hong Kong, our typical tea time was called dim sum. Historically, dim sum is a type of Chinese cuisine (predominantly Cantonese) that includes small bite-sized portions of food. There would be gigantic plates of very small food items – dumplings, vegetables, won tons, pastries, and steam buns plus more. Of course, all of this food was served with tea.

It is referred to as "going to tea" or yum cha that literally translates to "drink tea." However, there was certainly more eating in yum cha than drinking tea! There was no shortage of fried, steamed, or boiled foods. In yum cha, you'd to wait for a server to push their cart to you, announcing what types of food they had. A dim sum meal takes about an hour. While you were waiting for food to arrive and then eating when it did, there was always time to communicate.

When I traveled to California and had dim sum with relatives there, I began to realize how non-verbal my own immediate family was. My relatives were very different – cousins, aunts, and uncles who talked a lot... a lot more than we did. Dim sum was the perfect opportunity to communicate with each other rather than sit in silence after breaking out into an argument! My uncle never once shouted, "Stop talking and be quiet! No more talking." When I recall how my family was and see how we are now, I can see how tea has been very, very healing for us.

Tea and tea time definitely bring people together. Think about Victorian afternoon tea. That tradition started with Catherine of Braganza, the Portuguese wife of King Charles II. She is credited with introducing afternoon tea drinking to the British. The idea of tea time was widespread among Portuguese nobility. Her husband, the king, didn't spend much time with her, so she began spending afternoons with friends, enjoying small food items and pastries, like tappas, that stemmed from Portuguese culture... all while enjoying tea. And with that, the practice of serving and enjoying afternoon tea was born. With Hong Kong as a British port district, it's easy to see how the idea and practice of afternoon tea – ultimately dim sum – probably migrated back to the Canton area, in the same general region where tea originated in the first place.

Indeed, tea brings people together.

Giving Back to Community

As I've shared, part of my mission in launching my tea business was to promote and support the sense of community that I realized tea generated. Sipping Streams Tea Company is the official tea of the Yukon Quest – 1,000 Mile International Sled Dog

Race. As the name indicates, it's a 1,000-mile race between Fairbanks, Alaska and Whitehorse, Yukon Territory. The start location swaps each year, so every other year, it starts in my hometown of Fairbanks. About nine years ago, I stopped into the Yukon Quest office to offer a donation of tea for the event. The director immediately knew who I was. I'd had a show on the local classic rock radio station – "Tea on Tuesday" to teach about tea. Apparently, Fairbanks locals, including construction workers, dog mushers, truckers, etc. were listening and learning about tea.

Fairbanks has always been very community-oriented (in addition to being the dog-mushing capital of the world), and I wanted to be part of that. My tea donation offer was immediately and enthusiastically accepted. One caveat – make it really strong and make sure there's a lot of caffeine in it. Most mushers were coffee drinkers, so there were challenges to creating the right blend. First of all, it was a *race* that lasted up to 14 days, so mushers weren't going to take time to steep tea for very long. The blend included three high-end white and black teas that had a lot of caffeine. Actually, although most people believe the inverse to be true, white tea sometimes has more caffeine than black tea. However, I knew the mushers would associate boldness with caffeine and a really strong flavor. That's just the way our minds work. If the flavor wasn't strong, I thought the participants would be hesitant to drink it, thinking it didn't have much caffeine.

A very strong flavor would carry a more powerful psychological message. Additionally, the mind can also affect the impact of caffeine on the body – if you *think* there's a lot of caffeine, your body may possibly react accordingly. The placebo effect in action.

After the first year, several champion dog mushers really liked the beverage. They said it really worked and was easy to make while on the trail during the race. They could "throw it in and go." I'd designed the blend to be pretty foolproof. Let's face it – they weren't stopping for tea time in the middle of the wilderness and in the cold and snow, making a camp fire and timing the steeping! (Sometimes it was -40 to -60 degrees Fahrenheit in some locations). The tea was absolutely simple – instant and quick while tasting good and delivering caffeine. I chose teas that would never become bitter.

Later in the off-season, after the race had concluded, dog mushers and handlers started coming into the shop requesting this tea. However, I'd only designed it for the race and wasn't selling it in the store. We began custom blending it for them every time they came in. Before we knew it, the race rolled around again, and the Yukon Quest folks said, "You're definitely donating that tea again, right?"

Obviously, it was appreciated, and it really worked based on how I designed it.

Initially, I'd designed several versions of it and named it the "1,000 Mile Tea," hoping they would help me narrow down the best tasting recipe. Jamey, my assistant manager at the time, helped me fine-tune my 12 recipes down to six of them one evening, and he said he was only able to sleep for 30 minutes that night. Participants thought each of the six remaining versions tasted amazing. They certainly weren't tea connoisseurs. It was my job to give them what they needed in terms of good taste, easy to make, and plenty of caffeine along with the other inherent health benefits of tea.

The mushers in this race get very, very little sleep over the two weeks. It is not only the mushers who work long days with little sleep; the dog handlers do as well. The handlers drive hundreds of miles between remote checkpoints to meet their teams, clean after their teams, and take care of all the dropped dogs. The dog handlers also become pretty sleep deprived during the race.

This 1,000 Mile Tea was to be available for the handlers and volunteers as well as the mushers at every checkpoint along the race route. Sipping Streams Tea Company continues to donate tea and be a sponsor of this event.

After being a Yukon Quest sponsor for a few years, more and more people were hearing about this

1,000 Mile Tea and that you could only get it if you were somehow associated with the race – as a participant or volunteer. We finally decided to make it available for sale to the public. The testimonials of the mushers were really driving its popularity. They were blown away by the lack of jitters and stomach upset that usually comes with caffeine consumption and the acidity of coffee. It helped them get through 1,000 miles of mushing without the negative side effects that coffee can produce.

The folks who came in to buy 1,000 Mile Tea after we made it available to the public weren't buying it because they appreciated fine quality tea; they wanted a coffee alternative that could help them be more focused, stay awake longer, and avoid the jitters. Many of these people had doctors who were telling them to avoid coffee and switch to tea.

I was later interviewed on NPR about this tea, and in the middle of the interview when I explained what I'd created and why, a huge light bulb went off in my head: "This is exactly why everyone wants this tea – it's foolproof!" They could have a beverage that was easy to make and didn't give you the shakes. Even for folks not in the middle of a dog-mushing race, they could throw it in and go without worrying. It would taste amazing regardless.

There were many people who switched off Red Bull for this blend without even adding sugar. It's formulated to taste naturally sweet… just white tea and black tea. Now, it is one of our most popular blends, but the whole reason behind it was to support and bring recognition to both the Yukon Quest event and our community along with honoring those people who have the spirit to care for man's best friend, experiencing the beautiful aurora borealis while out on the trail in the middle of nowhere and the adventures they were sharing together.

Togetherness

As I said, tea brings people together – and sometimes in very unusual ways, whether they're in a tea shop, out on the trail, or simply around the dinner table.

No matter what type of person you are and what type of friends you have, you can easily and always start a conversation with another tea drinker. While I'm biased and stereotyping a bit, I'll say that tea drinkers are less irritable and grumpy. For them, it's never like "I have to have my tea!" the way that some coffee drinkers feel about that beverage... "Don't talk to me until I've had coffee."

People are not meant to be alone and isolated. Community is important, if not vital, to self-discovery, personal growth, realizing our potential, and influencing the world. I knew how important community was for *me*, so that's the reason I started my tea company. It quickly became obvious that tea was the medium that can bring together different people, different generations, and different cultures.

We are the average of the five people with whom we spend the most time. But how much actual face-to-face time do we spend with people anymore? In this fast-paced society, we barely have enough time for ourselves. Social media is undermining actual time spent together – physically present with one another. Do we even have time to process what we're going through every day? Or are we moving on to the next thing like a machine?

We're human beings, not robots, so we need others and long for intimacy – intimacy with others and even with ourselves to fully understand who we are and to be part of something greater than ourselves.

Like the people who come together and make up a community, there's a tea beverage that is made up of a community of microbes. That tea beverage is called kombucha. Kombucha is actually billions of microbes coexisting and working together. It is a symbiotic culture of bacteria and yeast that is started from a tea base. It is a variety of fermented, sweetened black or green tea drinks. Some people refer to it as a mushroom tea, but it's certainly not a mushroom. It gets the "mushroom" reference because of a disc that grows that looks like a mushroom or fungi. That disc is a highly concentrated, dense colony of bacteria and yeast coexisting.

Kombucha is touted for its health benefits. It's interesting that we have this great resource available to us that reflects what, as human beings, our hearts long for every day – to coexist in harmony and work together to create a better life.

Kombucha is powerful and works in and affects your gut. Historically, the ancients saw the bowel as the seat of human emotion:

"Greek poets, from Aeschylus down, regarded the bowels as the seat of the more violent passions such as anger and love, but by the Hebrews, they were seen as the seat of tender affections, especially kindness, benevolence, and compassion." (From etymonline.com)

In talking about stress and emotional turmoil, they were referring to their gut.

Think about it: When your gut doesn't feel well, everything else – including your attitude – is also upset and out of balance. The last time I personally had a tummy ache, I did not want to think about anything else but feeling better. I just wanted that tummy ache to pass by and end. The gut is the system in your body that is responsible for absorption and filtration; it is vital to your overall body health.

Your gut has a community of microbes working together. They're the probiotics in your intestines… a complex and diverse community of bacteria. This is why many people like to drink kombucha. In the same way that yogurt benefits your gut, so does kombucha. Kombucha is like a liquid probiotic. It can create and maintain balance in your internal system, starting in your gut.

Kombucha truly reflects human community. The microbes in kombucha are all different in the same way that we're all different (even if we live in the same community). Yet those microbes work together to achieve the necessary balance in the kombucha and in our bodies. Ideally, as humans, we'll all work together as well to achieve the harmony we're really designed to achieve.

To learn more, sign up for the Kombucha Culture course in which you'll learn more about it, what it does, how to flavor and store it, and what helps alter metabolism along with a variety of recipes. *http://bit.ly/learntea*

Chapter 7
The Tao of Tea & Mindfulness

A very large part of the idea of community is taking time... literally. Taking time to be with and support other people and ourselves. Slowing down and taking time is the foundation of truly being mindful. Mindfulness is a large part of stress reduction and overall well-being. When we slow down, we can literally make the time and space to be aware of where we are and what we're doing. When we're not physically moving around and doing things, we only have our minds to observe and process what's going on around us. Again, this is a critical component of both mental and physical health.

I grew up in a Buddhist family, although not one that was very strict in the practices... not so "orthodox," so to speak. However, my grandparents made a point to do tai chi every morning. After that, as I mentioned, my grandfather would then conduct his own Chinese tea ceremony. This ceremony reflects the central ideas of Taoism, Confucian, and Buddhism, being both a philosophy and a lifestyle. The ceremony – making tea, appreciating it, smelling tea, and enjoying tea – also underscores the importance of refreshing the mind and clearing the thoughts.

At the time, I didn't fully understand the ceremony. I always just thought, "It was Grandpa doing his tea thing" without understanding *why* he was doing it. Now I do understand the significance of making personal tea time just for yourself – to allow yourself to quietly be in the moment – rather than worrying about being productive or even talking to your best friend to catch up. This alone time is very important, and most people fail to make time… for themselves. We tend to make time for everything else but us.

I learned this vital lesson the hard way. At one point, I was in the emergency room three different times in two weeks, being completely out of work during that time. With every ER visit, the doctor would tell me that they only saw the symptoms I was exhibiting in people who were under incredible stress.

"Are you under a lot of stress?"

"Well… I don't think so.…" I was answering honestly. The pace I'd set in my life and the busy activity that came with running a business had become so normal to me that I did not recognize the level of stress I'd placed on myself. I was completely naïve and unaware of what my body was telling me. Clearly, mindfulness was lacking in my life. I didn't even take time to sit still for a minute. Work days were 16 hours long as I struggled to hold the business and everything else together. When I finally got home from a typical day, I went to bed and crashed, just to repeat the process the next day and the day after that and the day after that... and....

I never took time to think about myself. My body screamed, "Enough!" It got to the point that I couldn't even drink water; it burned my throat. I later discovered that my immune system was shot and I had lesions coating my throat. Add to that viral meningitis. All of this was my body's way to saying it was time to quit. If I wasn't going to choose to stop and take time for myself, my body was literally going to force it to happen. And it did.

The only thing I could drink was rooibos, as I shared in an earlier chapter. I knew how it worked as an anti-inflammatory. While I wasn't a big fan of the taste and did not prefer it, I did appreciate how it could help me. Drinking rooibos (because it reduced inflammation on contact in my throat) then allowed me to drink water without so much pain to stay hydrated and be able to swallow medications.

E+R=O

There are many things that happen in our lives, from simple things (like a broken toaster) to more serious problems (like my illness), that create stress and cause worry.

I recently learned an important lesson from Kent Julian, a renowned motivational speaker on leadership and productivity. According to Kent, we tend to believe that E=O, where E is the event and O is the outcome. If the event goes according to plan, the outcome will be good. However, if the event goes poorly, then the outcome is guaranteed to be negative. The problem with this equation is that you almost always end up with failure because events rarely go the way we want them to go. Events cannot be controlled.

Kent shares that there is a much better equation that you can adopt and buy into that almost always guarantees a successful outcome. In the new equation, add an R: E+R=O. The R represents our *response* and is the only thing over which we have total control. We can never control the events. When you own your response, you can take any event – even a very negative event – and turn it into a positive outcome. Choose to respond well. Choose to be better rather than bitter when facing a negative event.

This holds true no matter what you face in your life, but in order to own your response, you must be *mindful* of your response. As I mentioned, I had a whole series of negative events that occurred seemingly simultaneously... and if I'd only learned the E+R=O equation at that time, perhaps I wouldn't have continued to drive myself, even when my body started to shut down and forced me to stop... completely. During that stressful time and in the midst of the events I could not control, I'm not sure I was even eating one meal a day. The outcome was that I became sick enough to land in the ER on multiple occasions within a very short time. My mind still tried to focus on work, but my body screamed in reaction, "Absolutely not!" My body finally forced me to listen.

We must be aware and take time for mindfulness. If you are currently facing stressors or difficult events, I encourage you to immediately begin to listen to your body. It is telling you what you need. Own your response – the only thing you can control – and you can change the outcome to land in your favor. Be mindful!

Some think the tao of tea is like a religion, but I believe it is more of a philosophy of the way of tea. The way of tea is the daily practice of making tea for yourself or for someone else. In doing so, you take the time to be aware and be present in the moment that you are both making and enjoying the tea. My grandfather definitely had it right.

Being mindful is incredibly powerful. The most successful people and those with the most brilliant minds in the world always take time for reflection. Taking time for reflection is a choice. Speeding through each day, concentrating only on what you have to get done, is also a choice. Without time for reflection and stopping for a few minutes of mindfulness, how can we know where we are in life or where we're headed?

To alter Kent's equation just a bit, E+R=O, in which the R can easily stand for reflection. Without mindfulness and reflection, we cannot assess the current situation or event, so we cannot then tailor our response. Without our reflection and subsequent response, the outcome will be well outside our attempt to control it.

Conducting your own personal tea time, similar to the Chinese tea ceremony, is the perfect time to infuse a few minutes of quiet time into your day for reflection – time to consider where you are, what events are surrounding you, and what your response to those events should be.

I invite you to join The Essence of Tea. During this time, you will learn to improve your mindfulness about what the tea leaves look and smell like, how they unfurl in hot water, what the liqueur looks and tastes like. Once you learn to notice the details – and take time to do so – you will be on your way to becoming more mindful... to being in the moment, not only about tea but about everything around you.

Visit: http://bit.ly/learntea

Chapter 8

Gratitude

Growing up, my family tended to be unemotional. Very hardworking but simply not very demonstrative. As a young child of about four, I clearly remember giving my parents hugs and kisses before bedtime and sharing my "I love you's" as well. Typical for any 4-year-old and family. However, there came a point about three or four years later when those demonstrations and declarations of love and affection stopped. The love and affection did not end, simply the outward expression of it.

Perhaps I felt like part of the responsibility of growing up was to be less emotional. Hugs, kisses, and "I love you's" were something that babies and little kids did. I wanted to move beyond being a "little kid" and be more grown up. For whatever reason, my family no longer engaged in outward expressions of love and affection. Hugs and kisses went by the wayside. We even simply stopped saying "good night" to each other.

This is not necessarily cultural. My extended family was always emotionally expressive with one another. They never "outgrew" giving hugs to each other and wanting to be together. My cousins grew up in Hong Kong together and have always been very close. When I was in high school and met some of them for the first time in my life, I saw how they interacted with each other. It was very different from my own upbringing.

Whether the change in my immediate family about outward displays of affection was unspoken or the result of my assumption about being more grown up, I'm not sure. I simply did not express love with my family as I got older. Additionally, the words "thank you" weren't often said in our household. That's not to suggest we didn't have manners. I always said those words in public, at school, and at church but not at home. We weren't being rude to each other at home… simply unexpressive.

Apologies were also unspoken in our household. Like "thank you," "I'm sorry" was said to teachers, friends, etc., but not said to one another in my family. I rarely remember my parents using that phrase. As an observant child, I went with the flow and did and said (or didn't do and didn't say) what my parents did and said. They didn't say "thank you" or "I'm sorry," so neither did I when I was at home. Since they didn't say those phrases at home, I didn't think they were necessary, and we simply moved on.

This could have been encouraged by my father. He was the head of our household. Plus, he was the oldest of six other brothers and sisters. According to one aunt, "We never question what he says because he's the king of the family." I knew this was the attitude of my extended family and quite possibly the reason for the lack of expressed apology or gratitude from my father while I was growing up.

When I heard my aunt's comment during a family reunion after I'd graduated from college, my family's dynamic and unemotional approach to each other regarding love and affection started to make more sense. I gained a better understanding about why certain things weren't done in our family. My aunt had treated my father as "the king of the family," and my immediate family adopted the same approach. We never questioned what he did... or didn't do. Perhaps he should have been more demonstrative about his affection and gratitude and shared the occasional "I'm sorry," but he didn't and we followed his lead.

It wasn't the best example to follow. Thankfully, I was not isolated to my own immediate family. People at my church and friends and teachers at school also influenced me. The family dynamic was a conundrum: was it cultural or was it limited to my father? I had no idea as I started to try to understand who I was.

This became very bothersome about the time I was in college. Maybe everyone goes through this sort of struggle to understand who they are at this age. For me, it was an identity crisis – some saw me as too Chinese, some saw me as too "white" – coupled with my understanding of how I should receive love along with my own attitude.

At one point during college, I simply broke down. The relationships I developed at school were completely genuine, and these friends were so very thankful, honest, and encouraging. They sincerely wanted to listen to what I had to say. I couldn't get my head around that and felt that I did not deserve this level of friendship and love. It was inconsistent and incongruous with the way I grew up. To this point in my life, I hadn't had friendships that were that deep.

I questioned whether my friends' consistent expressions of gratitude or apologies were real or a point of manipulation. Did they *really* want to spend the time with me that they did? Or were they doing so because they wanted something from me besides friendship? I was learning how to trust people and how to openly receive love. It was one of the very biggest struggles I faced in college – far more challenging than any midterms or final exams. I didn't really know who I was.

The Most Important Lesson

This brings me to the important point of gratitude, and that was one of the most important things I learned in college. It takes time to dive into our turbulent emotions and dealing with those takes reflection. However, we only have time to reflect when we make time to reflect. This is why setting aside a personal intimate tea time is so important – it sets aside time for mindfulness.

Yes, it can be very messy to get into the heart of who we are and what is going on around us. We must take time to move beyond simple awareness. We need to reflect on our emotions and consider what we need to do with them and about them. We actually need to act on them.

We need to have gratitude about emotions, about the situation, and about everything. That is what seals the deal in us becoming truly whole. We need to accept what is and what has happened in our lives – both good and bad. We must accept even the things we don't really like about ourselves. We have to admit that we each have our own personal struggles with the different relationships we have or with the battle that goes on within us.

I'll be very open and share with you that I struggled greatly with depression in college… to the point that, on a few occasions, I actually thought about writing that "last final letter of goodbye to family and friends." Without fail, a friend would always call me just at the moment I was about to put pen to paper to say goodbye. It was absolutely God's will and a miracle because I would get this call every time I'd reached this very low point. I know God told my friend to call me at the very moment I needed to receive that call. My phone would ring (long before the days of cell phones), and the tone of her voice indicated to me that she knew exactly what was going on. I'd ask if she called because she knew how I was feeling and what I was contemplating. "No. I just wanted to call you and see how everything is going. You're my friend. I want to check up with you and spend time with you."

This was a shocker to me. We'd go on to talk about who I am, why she was thankful for me, and how I contributed to the friendship and the world. She would help me understand how my life and perspective were needed in this crazy world. This made me stop and think if I was truly thankful for everything in my life... thankful for all the relationships I have and the people who love me.

It is the most important lesson that I still practice. Do I take the time to say thank you for every little thing? Do I show my appreciation to Grandma Judy at church who never fails to tell me how glad she is to see me? Do I take the time to acknowledge when an aunt sends me a birthday card? Aunt Betty never fails to send me a card. It may seem like a simple little birthday card, but she's thinking about me and showing that she is thankful for me in her life.

It's an important lesson. I hope it is one that you will adopt and practice in your own life.

Gratitude and Goal Setting

Gratitude and goal setting fit together very nicely. Hand in glove, you might say.

Take time (and even put it on your calendar) to reflect on where you currently are and where you want to be. Of course, tea is optional but recommended during this reflection time! This includes thinking about your current place in both your career and personal life.

Consider the events of the past month and be grateful for each one of them. Have you owned your response to those events? If you've failed at that, think about how you could have changed your response for a better outcome and how you will handle it in the future.

Personally, I create a mind map each year with checkpoints at each month, mid-year, and the end of the year. During my own monthly checkup, I reflect on everything for which I'm thankful. I review and re-evaluate my goals – monthly goals, yearly goals, three-year goals, and lifetime goals. Sometimes goals change, and that is quite all right.

It is very important to take this time of, at least, monthly reflection. We often don't think about what we want because we are too focused on what we are doing instead. Being productive and "doing" is fine as long as you are doing something that is leading toward what you want in the first place. Simply "doing" without understanding why can be very stressful and isolating.

Every month, I reflect on what I'm thankful for, what things have gone right, and possibly what things have gone wrong. I find that when I do my own goal setting, gratitude helps me understand where I am and motivates me to reach my goals. On the other hand, this reflection time can help me decide when it's time to change goals as they evolve or become less important. Like I said, goals do change. For example, when I think about Grandma Judy at church, I am thankful that she's always so happy to see me; it reminds me that I need to recognize and show more love in my life. I'm encouraged every week I attend church. I'm loved and I am reminded to love.

Staying focused on gratitude while you're goal setting helps you really focus on what is important and what is not.

Take Action

When we take the time to reflect on all of the wonderful and positive things that have happened in our lives, our mindset and, in fact, this very world start to change. It doesn't end with mindfulness and awareness. It ends with action. Be proactive. Give back. Say the simple phrases of "thank you" and "I love you."

Inaction is a choice. Should you make the choice not to act, people and things will continue to move and will move on without you. Failure to act can, and often does, lead to missed opportunities. Be in the now and take time for intentional mindfulness and intentional action to express gratitude.

I thank God every day that my life has turned out the way it has… even through all the struggles. I can see how far I've come and how such a simple thing like tea has changed my life. God has put me in the place and position I'm in now – to positively affect the lives of other people around me. I'm also thankful for all of the positive influences of those who have always been there for me.

Things change, and while I will always be thankful for the road I've traveled because of tea, I may not always be on this particular road in the tea industry for the rest of my life. Even though we may hold something so dear to us, we cannot always hold on forever. Things don't always continue in a single direction, and things certainly don't move in a straight line. We must recognize this and appreciate it. Otherwise, when change invariably comes, it will seem devastating.

We need to be thankful for every small detail without holding on too tightly and without being inflexible and unwilling to budge. I believe God has put me where I am at every step in my life and has used tea as the industry of choice in which I could make a difference – it is what I'm supposed to do with my life. Yet I also recognize that there will be possible changes in the future, and I'm prepared for those. The same is true for you. You've been placed where you are for a purpose – the way in which you can make a difference in the world. Be mindful to recognize that but also be aware that it may change and evolve.

In the end, we all must be thankful for all of the small details and bigger events that have brought us this far and to the point at which we all are. This is not the end of my life, nor is it the end of yours yet. I'm not always certain of the exact path I should take, but I do know that every day I'll take time to express gratitude for everything for which I should be thankful. This is a huge aspect of being whole and happy. When I'm not in the mindset of gratitude, things seem very dark.

Be thankful every day because there is so much more to life than where we may be at any given time and what we're doing right now. We're not robots in our lives. We're not the "what." We are the "why." We're not simply what something is. I'm not just the "tea lady." We are each individuals with hearts, souls, and spirits.

Take time to reflect on your own *why* rather than *what* you are. You are here for a purpose. Sit with a cup of tea and discover what it is... today, tomorrow, and always.

Acknowledgments

In the spirit of gratitude, I'd like to thank you for taking the journey through this book with me. I'd also like to thank the following people who have contributed to this book and my life.

Even though I wanted to be a million different things when I was child, I never envisioned my life as a business owner, let alone a tea business owner. I want to thank my Savior for giving me this vision to share His love with the rest of the world through the medium of tea. Without him, none of this would be possible. Without His voice and clear path, I would have never done this.

To my spiritual family in Christ who were there for me since I was a child (the Harrises, the Changs, the Terhunes, and Ida Mae, Aunt Betty and Aunt Molly who have passed, and the rest of my UPBC family) and those who were with me in college (David and Keri Brown, Audra Olson, Cynthia Boline, Tara Maddox): thank you for showing me what it means to be loved and to accept love and encouragement. Through all my years of stubbornness, your unfailing love and patience is a true blessing that has helped me grow into the woman I am today.

To my intimate Sipping Streams family and friends, without you, none of this would be possible. You are the ones who have shaped my life and challenged me to be a leader through all my struggles. Your stories, your experiences, and your encouragement motivate me every day to continue the Sipping Streams mission. Thank you for all of your love and support throughout this tea journey. A special thank you to Jamey Wicklund, Joshua Amos, and Tara Miracle, who shaped my leadership and confidence in who I am as a boss and have put up with all my insecurities about myself – I am truly grateful for your patience and understanding. I honestly had no clue how to lead a team, but you believed in me and the mission of Sipping Streams; you always went above and beyond. Your silliness and unfailing support encouraged me every time I wanted to give up.

To my whole family from Hong Kong to New York. Thank you for supporting my crazy dream, even though tea traditionally in China is an "old person's" industry. Thanks for all the tea samples, tea pots, and stories about our family history. Thanks especially to yeh yeh (grandpa) who had "gung fu cha" every morning.

I am so thankful to have met so many amazing people through our local community, including the talented Whitney McLaren. Thanks for teaching me how to take aurora photographs between 2:00 and 4:00 a.m. at freezing temperatures (20° F) with glass and hot water. What an absolutely wonderful experience with light, patience, and natural beauty.

You had way more patience than I did when the Alaska State Trooper accosted us and ruined our best shots of the aurora borealis for the cover of this book. Thank goodness you took as many as we could on the icy cold ground. Do you normally get accosted by state troopers when you work for the Yukon Quest – 1,000 Mile International Sled Dog Race too? "Officer, we are just shooting pictures of a tea pot!"

And finally, to all my fans, customers, supporters, and TCB who believe in me and my dreams no matter what. My business and passion are not possible without you. I have seen you and your kids grow. I am excited and encouraged when you pass the tea passion onto others. I am amazed at seeing the transformational powers of tea in your life too!

Acknowledgements

What's Next:

Thank you for joining me as I've recounted my transformation journey. I hope I've inspired you to become more of a tea connoisseur as well.

I invite you to continue your own journey in the world of tea by connecting on social media:

Facebook:
https://www.facebook.com/sippingstreams

Instagram:
https://www.instagram.com/sippingstreams/

Twitter:
https://twitter.com/sippingstreams

YouTube:
https://www.youtube.com/channel/UCk3AQ4ivFie lwacIEF_-cOw?

Additionally, please consider subscribing to our newsletter and enrolling in one of our Universi-Tea courses to delve deeper into the incredible world of tea:

www.sippingstreams.com

What's Next

About the Author

Jenny Tse was born in Hong Kong but raised in Fairbanks, Alaska. Her vision for her company, Sipping Streams Tea Company, began in the summer of 2004 when she began to notice how tea brought different people together. A trip to China to further her education and her experiences as an entrepreneur inspired her to write *The Essence of Tea: The Transformational Journey of a Tea Connoisseur*.

Sipping Streams Tea Company has been featured in *Fresh Cup Magazine* and *Edible Alaska*.

Tse is a certified tea specialist with the Specialty Tea Institute, and her blends have won numerous top prizes at the North American Tea Championships and Global Tea Championships. She has also been a featured speaker at the World Tea Expo and won first place for the Top Tea Infusionist Competition at the World Tea Expo in 2011.

Made in the USA
Middletown, DE
24 May 2021